A COLORING BOOK
BASED ON A COURSE IN MIRACLES
COLORFUL WISDOM FOR SPIRITUAL TRANSFORMATION

ILLUSTRATED BY ANDREA SMITH

BEYOND WORDS
Hillsboro, Oregon

BEYOND WORDS

Beyond Words Publishing
20827 N.W. Cornell Road, Suite 500
Hillsboro, Oregon 97124-9808
503-531-8700 / 503-531-8773 fax
www.beyondword.com

First Beyond Words trade paperback edition July 2016

Beyond Words Publishing is an imprint of Simon & Schuster, Inc. and the Beyond Words logo is a registered trademark of Beyond Words Publishing, Inc.

For more information about special discounts for bulk purchases, please contact Beyond Words Special Sales at 503-531-8700 or specialsales@beyondword.com.

Manufactured in the United States of America

10 9 8 7 6 5 4 3 2 1

ISBN 978-1-58270-630-6

The corporate mission of Beyond Words Publishing, Inc.: *Inspire to Integrity*

This coloring book is dedicated to the people of our planet who want love and peace. We must create the "feeling" in ourselves if we want to anchor the feeling on Earth. We can create our very own paradise on Earth by living a life full of love. The only way we will create the loving vibration is by embracing it and being it.

{ FOREWORD }

We have known Andrea Smith for over thirty years. Her paintings and philosophy have always embraced the principles of *A Course in Miracles*. The feeling of peace is evident in her work and that is what she wishes to share and express from her heart.

Usually Andrea's paintings are all strong lines and vibrant in color, but in this book everything has been reduced to black lines to be colored in. The message of peace within is still clear even within the line drawings. Andrea's work reminds us to look deep within ourselves if we want the peace that God gives us.

Meditation is one way of stilling our mind. The act of coloring and creating can put us in a similar state of relaxation and calm. Andrea has found a way to combine activity and quiet time to create a peaceful state of mind.

—Dr. Gerald G. Jampolsky and Dr. Diane Cirincione

{ INTRODUCTION }

I created this unique coloring book based on *A Course in Miracles*, which is a spiritually oriented text that has shaped and defined my life for over 35 years. Each spread—consisting of a lesson and my original artwork—is meant to be an observational meditation while you engage in the act of coloring.

The lessons are meditations in themselves and the act of coloring in the images while meditating on the words is a powerful practice. Between the images and the words a unique dynamic is set up to increase the quality of the experience. As one meditates on the words a deep understanding can be reached and the feeling becomes anchored in our being.

The intention of the coloring book is to offer the feeling of peace to the person engaged with it. As I have learned from *A Course in Miracles*, peace on Earth begins with peace within. Heaven is not a place but more of a state of awareness that all is perfect in this instant and this is all there is. Perfect oneness. And the imagery in this book is about the most important relationship we have, the one with ourselves.

The female and male images throughout are actually referring to each side of our brain. The right side or the *intuitive* is the female side. The left or *logical* is the male side. In order to function fully in a balanced way, we must use both sides. We have Mother Earth and Father Sky reminding us of this balance daily. My hope is that the take away from using this coloring book is an ultimate feeling of peace within oneself. The act of coloring, which engages our entire body—emotional, physical, ethereal, and spiritual—leaves us in a state of bliss. The reason is because we are satisfied and "no body" is left out.

I believe it is up to us to create the world we want to live in. We are the ones to hold a higher vision and gentler consciousness. The cherubs I draw remind us to rise above petty, seemingly difficult experiences. The key is to constantly begin again and show up renewed. Being present is a huge part in living a peaceful life. Allowing the time to color these pages and really reflect on the messages will guarantee peace. If you are willing to embrace the principles of *A Course in Miracles* and use them, your world will be brighter and lighter!

{Lesson 15}

My thoughts are images that I have made.

{Lesson 23}

I can escape from the world I see by giving up attack thoughts.

{Lesson 27}

Above all else I want to see.

{Lesson 29}

God is in everything I see.

{Lesson 30}

God is in everything I see because
God is in my mind.

{ LESSON 34 }

I could see peace instead of this.

{LESSON 37}

My holiness blesses the world.

{ LESSON 41 }

God goes with me wherever I go.

{Lesson 43}

God is my source.
I cannot see apart from Him.

{Lesson 44}

God is the light in which I see.

{LESSON 45}

God is the Mind with which I think.

{Lesson 46}

God is the Love in which I forgive.

{Lesson 47}

God is the strength in which I trust.

{LESSON 49}

God's Voice speaks to me all through the day.

{LESSON 50}

I am sustained by the Love of God.

{LESSON 61}

I am the light of the world.

{Lesson 66}

My happiness and my function are one.

{LESSON 67}

Love created me like itself.

{Lesson 74}

There is no will but God's.

{Lesson 92}

Miracles are seen in the light,
and light and strength are one.

{LESSON 93}

Light and joy and peace abide in me.

{LESSON 101}

God's Will for me is perfect happiness.

{Lesson 108}

To give and to receive are one in truth.

{Lesson 109}

I rest in God.

{LESSON 121}

Forgiveness is the key to happiness.

{ LESSON 122 }

Forgiveness offers everything I want.

{Lesson 126}

All that I give is given to myself.

{Lesson 127}

There is no love but God's.

{ LESSON 135 }

If I defend myself I am attacked.

{Lesson 141}

My mind holds only what I think with God.

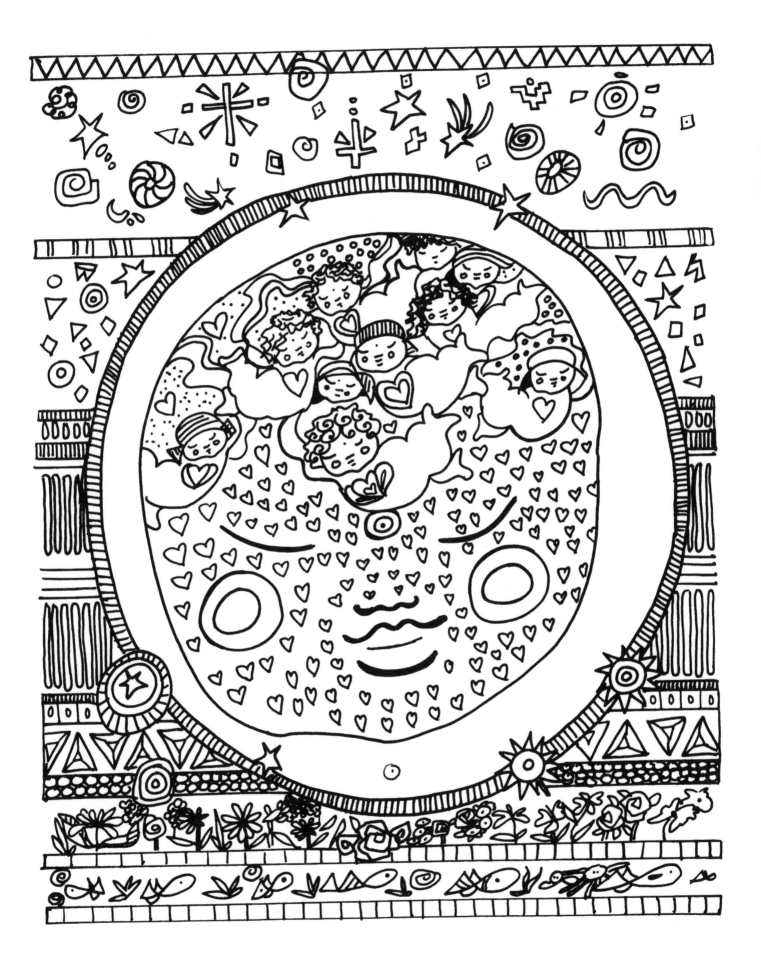

{Lesson 185}

I want the peace of God.

{LESSON 188}

The peace of God is shining in me now.

{LESSON 189}

I feel the love of God within me now.

{Lesson 194}

I place the future in the Hands of God.

{Lesson 195}

Love is the way I walk in gratitude.

{Lesson 199}

I am not a body, I am free.

{Lesson 200}

There is no peace except the peace of God.

{LESSON 221}

Peace to my mind.
Let all my thoughts be still.

{LESSON 229}

Love, which created me, is what I am.

{Lesson 225}

This day I choose to spend in perfect peace.

{Lesson 264}

I am surrounded by the Love of God.

{Lesson 265}

Creation's gentleness is all I see.

{LESSON 267}

My heart is beating in the peace of God.

{LESSON 270}

I will not use the body's eyes today.

{LESSON 273}

The stillness of the peace of God is mine.

{Lesson 286}

The hush of Heaven holds my heart today.

{Lesson 290}

My present happiness is all I see.

{ Lesson 291 }

This is a day of stillness and peace.

{LESSON 293}

All fear is past and only love is here.

{Lesson 297}

Forgiveness is the only gift I give.

{Lesson 308}

This instant is the only time there is.

{Lesson 309}

I will not fear to look within today.

{LESSON 314}

I seek a future different from the past.

{ LESSON 336 }

Forgiveness lets me know
that minds are joined.

{Lesson 346}

Today the peace of God envelops me,
and I forget all things except his love.

{ ACKNOWLEDGMENTS }

This happens to be the 50TH anniversary of *A Course in Miracles*. I am forever indebted to this book for reminding me everyday that love is always the answer, no matter the question or challenge I face.

The first people I want to thank (although I never actually met them), must be Helen Schucman and William Thetford. These two people channeled and transcribed the entire *A Course in Miracles* book. Helen heard the voice and William supported her because they wanted peace for everyone.

Next, I want to thank Dr. Gerald Jampolsky and his wonderful wife, Dr. Diane Cirincione. It was Jerry who introduced me to the course through his books. Jerry and Diane teach and live "the course" daily—moment to moment. I love them dearly and they inspire and uplift so many with their lives.

Then there is Richard and Michele Cohn, owners of Beyond Words Publishing. They are my dear friends and such incredible visionaries. It was Michele who loved the idea of this coloring book and made it happen! None of this book would have come together without the expertise of Lindsay Brown of Beyond Words. Thank God she was there!

Last, and certainly not the least is my family. My son Matthew and his wife Kriston are such loving and wonderful parents to my grandsons Sky and Jet. My daughter Lindsey is an incredible mother and it is reflected in my granddaughter Lexi. They are the reasons I began to read *A Course in Miracles*, so I want to thank them for inspiring me to want to see another way.

My final tribute is to my husband Gary. He has always been my biggest supporter throughout my career and it is also our fifty-year wedding anniversary this year. My heart is filled with gratitude and appreciation for all of the incredible love and energy I have received throughout this process.